10 IMPROVISATIONAL CLARINET ETUDES
by Jeff Coffin

ISBN 9781953622020
Copyright © 2020 by Jeff Coffin. All rights reserved.
No part of this book may be duplicated or shared without the permission of Jeff Coffin.

Also available online as an e-book.
Special thanks to Josh Karas for his assistance.
Layout and cover design by Robert Hakalski.
Engraving by Kyle Gordon.
Back cover photo courtesy of Jeff Coffin.
www.jeffcoffin.com/clarinet

WELCOME!

I am primarily an improvising saxophonist but I also play quite a bit of flute and clarinet. While I'm not really interested in being a classical flute or clarinet player, I appreciate that the classical repertoire builds a strong foundation. However, finding non-classical studies to play that more suit my wants and needs are hard to find. I figured others might be having a similar issue so I made some up!

What you have here are ten improvisational clarinet etudes. I originally played and then transcribed them on flute (available as *10 Improvisational Flute Etudes*) but they work great for clarinet too! **I have provided free MP3 streaming and downloads at www.jeffcoffin.com/clarinet** so you can hear and get a feel for the solos. They are played by the amazing James Zimmermann (Principal Clarinetist/Nashville Symphony 2008-2020).

If you want to play through them with backing tracks, which is best, I recommend getting the iRealPro app so you can change the various settings to your liking. If this is already a familiar musical language and style for you, choose your own tempo and just start playing. If not, please listen to the examples and try to imitate. I recommend taking them quite slowly at first and eventually build them up to an excruciatingly fast tempo that makes your key joints smoke from the friction!! Well, I **DO** recommend starting slowly.

These solo etudes are improvisations I played using iReal Pro. I recorded into Pro Tools, transcribed my solos (tip: get the rhythms first if you're writing down solos), made some edits, put them into Sibelius, had someone fix the errors I made putting them into Sibelius, re-recorded them with the corrections and edits, and now they are ready to be played. Easy! :-)

I chose the chord changes to standard jazz repertoire that I thought would be familiar, beneficial, and fun to play. I think this book has something for everyone. Oh, and I named the solos just for fun.

Some of these might be pretty challenging but it's always good to have things to work on that take some extra effort. I wouldn't want you to be bored.

The recorded tempos are for example only so it doesn't matter if you play them slower to faster than the recording on your own. Find tempos that work for you and that allow you to sound good and execute the material.

I hope you have a fun time with these and that you learn some things along the way. I know I did. Good luck!

Peace, JC

jeffcoffin444@gmail.com
www.jeffcoffin.com/clarinet

TABLE OF CONTENTS

Etudes in the Lower Register

4-6 **Olive Mi** = All of Me
7 **Space Flies Like Star Pies** = Star Eyes
8-11 **Bluetude** = Blues (B♭ & C concert)
12-13 **It's The Little Things** = All The Things You Are
14-15 **Mrs. Kowalski** = Stella By Starlight
16-17 **The Answer Is Yes!** = Confirmation
18-20 **The Jones Tones** = Have You Met Miss Jones
22-23 **It's Only You** = There Will Never Be Another You
24-25 **King Of Leaps** = Giant Steps
26-27 **Where My Photos At?** = Someday My Prince Will Come

Etudes in the Higher Register

30-32 **Olive Mi** = All of Me
33 **Space Flies Like Star Pies** = Star Eyes
34-37 **Bluetude** = Blues (B♭ & C concert)
38-39 **It's The Little Things** = All The Things You Are
40-41 **Mrs. Kowalski** = Stella By Starlight
42-43 **The Answer Is Yes!** = Confirmation
44-46 **The Jones Tones** = Have You Met Miss Jones
48-49 **It's Only You** = There Will Never Be Another You
50-51 **King Of Leaps** = Giant Steps
52-53 **Where My Photos At?** = Someday My Prince Will Come

"If you're a clarinet player and you're looking for a fun challenge that will help you get more comfortable with improvisation, look no further! Jeff has put together a fun collection of etudes that'll stretch your ear and help you understand the structure of a well-improvised solo. You'll explore a wide range of styles and you'll emerge with more confidence in your own abilities. And you'll be whistling the the tunes for weeks!"

James Zimmerman
Principal Clarinetist / Nashville Symphony (2008-2020)

"I really enjoyed your book of études and plan to use them with students.

Greg Tardy
Saxophonist/Clarinetist / Professor of Saxophone, University of Tennessee, Knoxville TN

Jeff Coffin's Improvisational Etudes for Clarinet are a great resource for classical teachers and students looking for a way to introduce the improvisational style into their playing. The etudes are written in a way that allows us to see clearly into the mind of a great improviser, while being accessible enough for the classically trained clarinetist to perform without fear!

Bixby Kennedy
Associate Principal Clarinetist of the New Haven Symphony Orchestra,
Associate Principal in the Albany Symphony, Principal Clarinetist of Symphony in C,
Professor of Clarinet / Vanderbilt University

OLIVE MI
All of Me

Comp. **Jeff Coffin**

SPACE FLIES LIKE STAR PIES
Star Eyes

Comp. **Jeff Coffin**

BLUETUDE
Blues in C

Comp. **Jeff Coffin**

-8-

BLUETUDE

BLUETUDE
Blues in D

Comp. **Jeff Coffin**

IT'S THE LITTLE THINGS
All The Things You Are

Comp. **Jeff Coffin**

MRS. KOWALSKI
Stella By Starlight

Comp. **Jeff Coffin**

MRS. KOWALSKI

THE ANSWER IS YES!
Confirmation

Comp. **Jeff Coffin**

THE ANSWER IS YES!

THE JONES TONES

Have You Met Miss Jones

Comp. **Jeff Coffin**

-18-

THE JONES TONES

THE JONES TONES

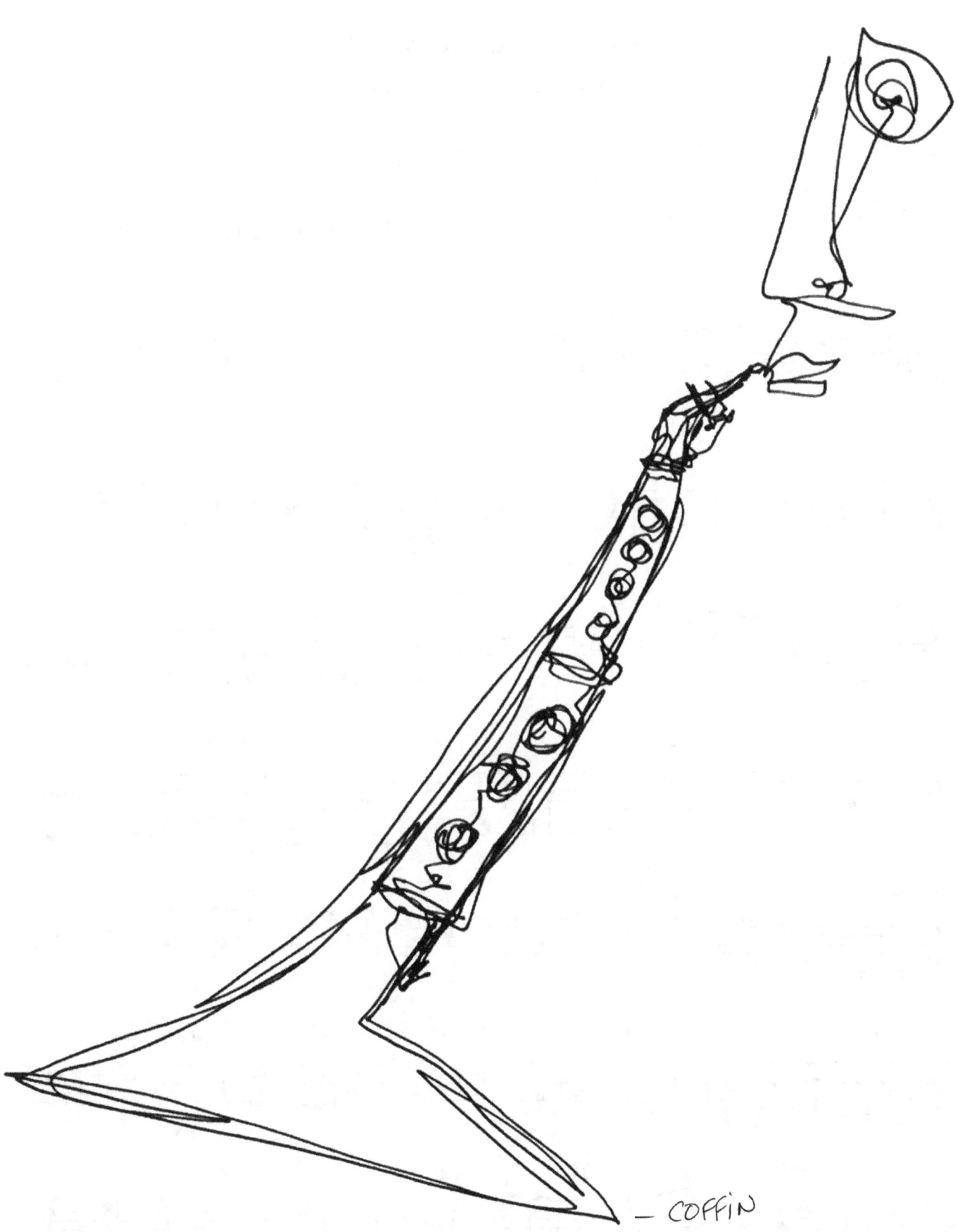

IT'S ONLY YOU
There Will Never Be Another You

Comp. **Jeff Coffin**

KING OF LEAPS
Giant Steps

Comp. **Jeff Coffin**

KING OF LEAPS

WHERE MY PHOTOS AT?

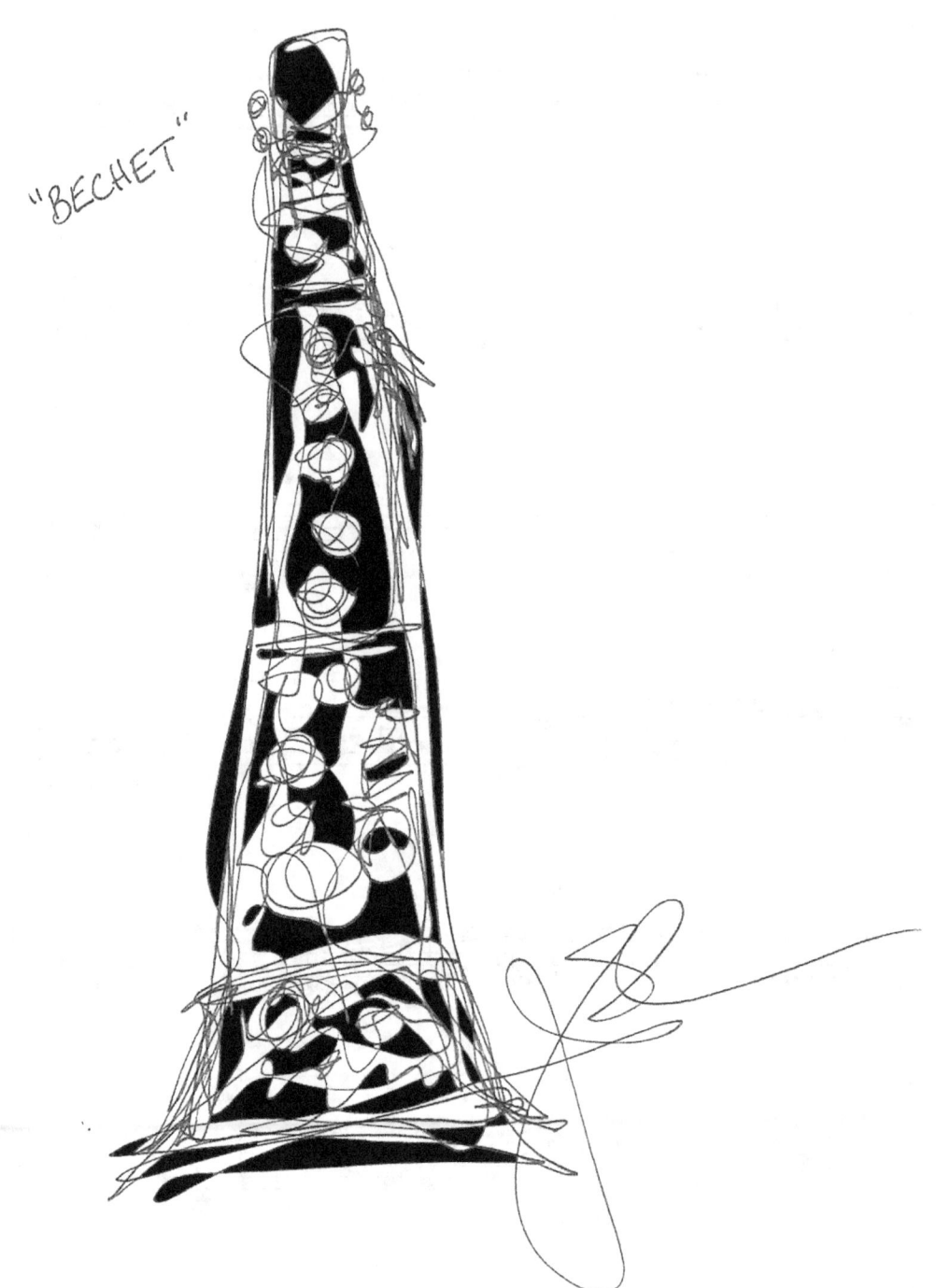

Here are the etudes in the upper register.
Most everything has been transposed up with the exception of any notes above the high G.
It's best not to tempt fate. :)

Great clarinet players like Artie Shaw, Benny Goodman, Jimmy Hamilton, Buddy DeFranco,
Eric Dolphy, Don Byron, Anat Cohen, Eddie Daniels, etc…all spend a lot of time playing in this register.
Both registers are challenging and have their merits of course.

HAVE FUN!

OLIVE MI
All of Me

Comp. **Jeff Coffin**

SPACE FLIES LIKE STAR PIES
Star Eyes

Comp. **Jeff Coffin**

fine

BLUETUDE
Blues in C

Comp. **Jeff Coffin**

BLUETUDE

BLUETUDE
Blues in D

Comp. **Jeff Coffin**

BLUETUDE

IT'S THE LITTLE THINGS

MRS. KOWALSKI
Stella By Starlight

Comp. **Jeff Coffin**

MRS. KOWALSKI

THE ANSWER IS YES!
Confirmation

Comp. **Jeff Coffin**

THE ANSWER IS YES!

THE JONES TONES
Have You Met Miss Jones

Comp. **Jeff Coffin**

THE JONES TONES

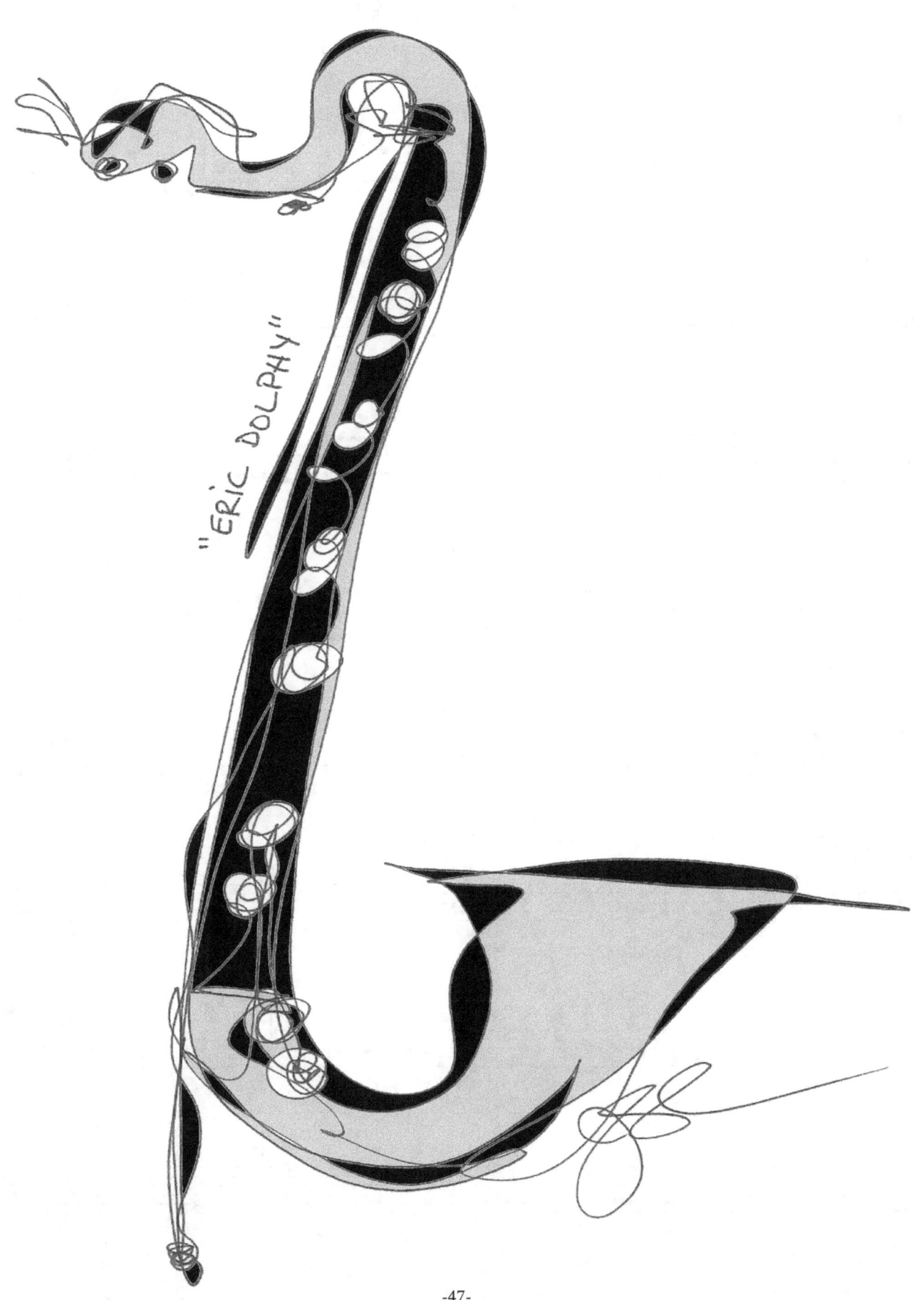

IT'S ONLY YOU
There Will Never Be Another You

Comp. **Jeff Coffin**

-48-

IT'S ONLY YOU

KING OF LEAPS
Giant Steps

Comp. **Jeff Coffin**

KING OF LEAPS

WHERE MY PHOTOS AT?
Someday My Prince Will Come

Comp. **Jeff Coffin**

-52-

WHERE MY PHOTOS AT?

ALSO BY JEFF COFFIN

10 Improvisational Flute Etudes
The Road Book
The Saxophone Book (1-3)
Jeff Coffin & the Mu'tet Play-Along
The Articulate Jazz Musician (w/Caleb Chapman)

Available at www.jeffcoffin.com

- NOTES -

www.ingramcontent.com/pod-product-compliance
Lightning Source LLC
Chambersburg PA
CBHW081158070526
44583CB00021B/2903